in the dark times
oakley

First published in March 2018 by Black Pear Press
www.blackpear.net

Copyright © Oakley Flanagan 2018

ISBN 978-1-910322-59-8

Cover design by Black Pear Press

dedication

for Kitty Connelly
but also   for you

In the dark times
Will there also be singing?
Yes, there will also be singing.
About the dark times.

Bertolt Brecht
from 'Motto'

No man is an island,
Entire of itself,
Every man is a piece of the continent,
A part of the main.

If a clod be washed away by the sea,
Europe is the less.
As well as if a promontory were.
As well as if a manor of thy friend's
Or of thine own were:

Any man's death diminishes me,
Because I am involved in mankind,
And therefore never send to know for whom the bell tolls;
It tolls for thee.

John Donne
1624

testimonials

"oakley's considered words speak beautifully of the belligerence that has become our everyday. It is epic in its ache and soothing in its soulfulness."
—**Sabrina Mahfouz**

"truthful, damning, cathartic.
oakley's collection speaks of the rotting mulch we live in, hoping for new shoots to sprout."
—**Polarbear**

"a precious work holding an energy that makes the reader exhale in awe between each poem; oakley is really something."
—**Caleb Femi—Young People's Laureate for London**

about oakley

oakley is a poet, playwright, writer and performer from the West Midlands and is a former Worcestershire Young Poet Laureate (2017). oakley has worked with the Birmingham Rep and Theatre Royal Stratford East writing for theatre and performance and had work produced and read in Birmingham and London; recently for theatre *the kill list* (Southwark Playhouse, Little Pieces of Gold), *pray your wings will carry you* produced by Full Disclosure Theatre Company and *nibling* for The MONOBOX's inaugural playwrighting development programme: PlayStart. oakley was longlisted for the Outspoken Prize for Page Poetry in 2016 and later published by Hashtag Queer in America for 2016's LGBTQ+ creative anthology. A member of Apples and Snakes' 2017 Writing Room for emerging poets and also a member of the National Youth Theatre of Great Britain, oakley is currently working on another collection whilst continuing to write for theatre.

contents

prelude (to terror)

our Mother
Earth

brittle arthritic bones
calcified by her age
cracking all around
like porcelain

see her
        appraise her features
        surveying the extent of her body

bloated and bleeding
back broken by the weight of her burden

anorexic stomach   eating itself
until her mouth heaves   bulimic
spilling the contents of our waste

the bombs at her spine
the lights flickering in her eyes
the politician's words
poison her mouth

her speech stolen
shell-shocked silence
indignantly resigned
to our fate

watch her   unfold herself
exhale the fumes   like a smoker

the oceans boil   as she stifles a scream
in her cold   tired   breath

as she watches
sister Moon
like a bouquet of lilies
held by the sky
at the graveside
of her fallen children

2.22 am

it's 2.22 am and i wake hot from another nightmare that sees my city eat
itself whole

regurgitate the bones to fossilise

become a footnote in the history of time

i sit in the pregnant darkness

allow the seconds to recalibrate

focus

> note the absence of natural sound
> the low artificial drum that hums from all that is man-made

the boiler halts   the loaded clock outruns itself

> the last of the drunks rebuke the night's faux-gold
> gilded promise

> > tramps seek refuge in the doorway of some richer
> > home

> > > or take residence in silence forsaken on a
> street corner

and i get up   stand

before the window   cower from the edge of the
        glass

(in case for some reason   somehow   someone is up this late and
catches my eye   and we are both forced to confront this   *loneliness*)

it's only drizzling but from inside the rain sounds like
    it's pelting

everything is magnified

above   the sky

cracked   to make way for morning

looks like it will give way to thunder at any moment   split
    itself in half

roar   pour forth the last down-pour to wash
    us away
                        bring us back to ourselves

and there is this space i've never been before

a gap a void   that calls to be filled or at least
reconciled with

but it's too late and i've got work in the morning so i
    draw the curtains

                        try to get some sleep

dredging

i am so tired
        i want to sleep
            but the memory of our past

                is dredging the water

            bringing all that we drowned
            back to the surface

4

it's always at night when the visions come

ships sway in the wind
knock against the walls of the border
the last teenager alive
streams their suicide on Facebook
an eagle spreads its wings
like a bomber over europe
as the swan sits mute in the water

hurricanes

plastic red roses in fumigated underground bunkers
howl quiet mourning in this impregnable fortress

there is no wind here
no flowers grow
they just blister

the camp from long ago
they used to say served as a reminder
that inhumanity such as that
defiled even nature
by the fact that no birds flew above
must never happen again
they said
but that was years back
before the developer sold it for real estate

and once more
the flowers protest
they will not grace this wretched place
with their rich colour anymore

the future is muted
the story is familiar
we will never learn

we are hurricanes   in our paths
only preserved   then turn in on ourselves
by our constancy   and collapse
to destroy all things

crumble

colourless eyes too collapse
into bloodless sockets

legs melt
their thunder lost

smiles drop to frowns
and gums rot in tobacco

eyes dim
    dulled

wasted brains reel
in smack and speed
    immobilised

gone are the days of pure forms
buried in landslides of anaesthetic excesses

this is a new kind of slavery

dreams
turn to dust

unguarded minds go to slop
and bodies finally

implode

mourning

the morning is illuminating
concrete brick roadways
London is re-birthing itself again

slowly   and then all at once

the morning is crying   realising you're gone
the tube jolts hesitantly   just waiting
morning has a concise hope   before

each early bus   rushed breakfast   first fag of the day
killing us both   a little more
                                            slowly

the sun is up not shining   vomiting
whole portions of light across the landscape
revealing all the places you're absent from

.

commute

caught in last night's insomnia
and this morning's early shift
music in my mind
melody of rarely heard peace
amidst this violent chaos

old woman buried alive in her shopping

young girl buried alive in her reflection

a heavy pram with a dodgy wheel

a bike with a broken chain
have to be pushed the rest of the way

the lights are always this bright
no matter the time of day

lager screams rudely at 7 in the morning

poor kid cowers behind toilet door
shirks card machine
and unsympathetic conductor

the disaster of all these tiny   quiet lives

doors open
suits swarm
coffee cups quiver
under the strain

private school children
packed tight like disproportionate statistics

they shun unoccupied seats beside shop assistants
hug the doors ready to exit

and they laugh with one another
making jokes in dead Latin

the air turns palpable and thick
soured

wage

the hours of your life it takes to earn the tokens
that barely stretch to keep you alive and pay your rent

on my way home

i walk the city guided by artificial streetlights
under a star-plucked sky
above is empty

i navigate miles of unbroken black tarmac
under a sky that used to have tiny lights in it
and i think of lost lovers

as strangers
thick with the narrative of their own heavy lives
walk past me without even glancing

if even the stars have left us
what hope do we have?

mad again

rocket man on *a suicide mission*
says orange man with his mercury tongue

men with their fingers hovering over the button
citizens looking away from the sun
anticipating the shadow

night in
in front of the atrocity box

glued to flooding feeds
cyclical newspeak
slack jawed   shaking
before the TV's backlight
caught in the inactive cripple of glow
trying to process all this inhumanity

amoeba

the political policy of isolationism has become startlingly present in our
personal lives
heads bowed down
to our phones
in the hope we won't notice the blood on our hands

the honeyed drippings of monotony

today the same as tomorrow tomorrow like yesterday yesterday like all
the other days

    the honeyed drippings of monotony
    clogging up my soul
    weighing down my wings

incorporeal

when the curtains are drawn
and the likes dry up

when the night draws
in
and your eyes
adjust to that
unfriended darkness

you catch your own reflection
and look away fast

unsure of what you see

adam

dancing around   in our cardboard fantasy   feels like
we're in some shitty reality show
the ones that you watch   not sure if it's real or
not like a video game
                  sometimes I feel that
my life is a video game   pixel zombies coming at me from all angles

             trying to eat my brains out
and it's strange   the things I stare at
                through the screen
                look more appealing
the apple seems so much more appetising
the way it shines in high-definition
all that is real is just grey
                but that thing in my hand it glows brighter
                than the chrome its warmth emanates from
it promises me so much
            so much
                      like a wallflower that
                 somehow blooms in the dark
and that's fucking mental

             there's this part of me   been niggling away at
       me   for years
an ocean just wearing me down
                  every morning I wake up
                  before I get out of bed
                  before I get dressed to go to
                  work

     I can see ghosts at the foot of my bed just staring at me

not saying a word

        but piercing right through my soul with their
            eyes

I haven't told my girlfriend yet   'cause I'm scared

and 'cause I know it's my fault
        it's all my fault

the perfect construction of you

to truly see the state of things would end you
so you sit in the glow of the screen's perfect promise
instead

let's face it the world outside is fucked   why not embrace what
    makes us so modern?
it's softer here   things see more honest
somehow

to truly feel the weight of our ceaseless inhumanity cuts too deep
so you scroll
and scroll
and scroll
and scroll

too much to feel
too many dead
too soon
(anytime is too soon)

the drones the blood the bones the bombs the deadlines the doubt
churning in your belly like a bad pill

too much to grasp
so sit in the glass tower of your greatest victory
behold   the perfect construction of you

feel your pained bruised heart comforted by the smooth edges of digital
prison blocks
construct a life built on the conceit that you'll somehow be closer to
everyone
then complain that you feel lonely

the crippling loneliness

sometimes I feel like I'm living in a computer game
it's like nothing feels

      real

what use is a heart
when there are filters and lights and perfection everywhere?
a bright 24-hour promise

smiles rehearsed before cold glass in bathrooms
whose toilets act as the stomachs for the young
starving themselves aspirational
hiding in the illusion of their perfect self

all smiles and photos of extravagant meals
left for the sparrows to peck at

so don't kill us
control us
divide us
or distract us
we'll do that for ourselves

no guns no violence
no shooting of activists
just give us a newsfeed
and we'll do the rest ourselves
as we assemble other happier selves online
birch trees to seek shade
from the glare of the corporate sun

the image of another dead refugee
another black child shot in a gutter

white fist black glove
becomes cannonfodder
for another armchair activist
as they reload the gun
click bait for an undying racist
another black body bleeding into the intersection of a street gutter and
police car
is swiped past

so please
give us filters
to block it all out

give us memes
and hashtags
to bury ourselves

give us somewhere to spend hours doing nothing
to fill that hole inside of us which is seeking something
to quiet the scream

give us nothing

add
request
accept
     like
snap
filter
upload
take down
change filter
re-upload
     like
share
       scroll
purge
censor
ignore
spout
chastise
cloy
     like   share
scroll
scroll
scroll
[repeat]

eve

about the only time he talks is when he's half-cut
coming in from work I'll find him sat here
with the lights out
just sitting
hasn't even looked for jobs
not even turned the laptop on
doesn't wanna try and find work
says there's no point
says it means nothing
says he wants to be free a free man

I say free?
what's free got to do with it
nothing's free

one day I came home from work
and found him in the kitchen with a blackbird and a steak knife
he'd cut its wings off
bits of blood and feathers everywhere
I said what the fuck d'you think you're doing?
and he looked at me
and said
I just didn't think it was fair

distance

we find ourselves in days made   wide   by the distance
that only   thunderstorms or earthquakes
                        or bombs or falling buildings
can bring us back
together

a frailty
only this fault line can expose

old woman #1

just sat here on my own   waiting for it to ring
                            ring ring   ring ring

                            hello mum   hello nan we love you we're
                            coming over

                            they'll find me like this
                            one morning

                            the post-man will smell me through the
                            letterbox
                            knock the door down

I'll be here   a frightening fossilised thing
                            all bone
                            and dust
                            hand outstretched to the phone   still
                            waiting

out of nature

enchained in the days
the way solitary birds look
when crouched upon
telephone poles
somehow out of nature

where each day rises incurable
gives way to hours of screens and scrolling
listless taps that sound frantic

the culture is shipwrecked
upon some far off Island
we still call Great
with the last of what burns
smouldering

the stillness of the hour
gives way to the day
this tired skin
rushes to rot
but you must seek out patience from
    the years
forfeit the chattering screen
for something more honest

i listen to the few populated trees
that somehow still sing
as if their world hadn't already ended

she

    adds a mound of sugar to her cappuccino
    cuts the cake into segments
    offers me a slice

she
    stirs her coffee
    tonight's late shift
    heavy under her eyes

she
    sips and after
says
        I worry for him
        sometimes I say to myself
        what on earth have you brought him into?
        and I feel so selfish

she
    places her coffee cup down
    shakes her head
    and stares at me

her eyes
two weeping sores

        I do worry for him

she says

        all I've got left is the worry
        I worry all the time

(poppies at least are flourishing
even in warzones)

sow seeds in this wasteland of our days
so that that flowers might grow
(poppies at least are flourishing
even in warzones)

unplug the charger
drain the battery
shut the screen down forever

find me in a room that hums with electricity
and fill the blank sound in with sand

offer me a deep ocean
a new moon
something in all this nothing

give me soil
give me charcoal
give me wood
give me blood

just give me something real

lay down next to me   imperfect
terrified   awake
and lift me high
in the hope
i might fly   far

bad kid

you are a bad kid   nothing but your mouth
             an open wound filled full of salt by God
you
with all your nonchalance
and that supercilious manner

your mother does not believe you when you tell her why you were so
late
your father says little
because he knows where you have been   he's been there too

everything is bullshit
everyone is so full of pretence
apart from you of course

and so
when you meet him
and he is just like you
sees the world in exactly the same way
there grows a softness in your chest that you have never known

you both look up to the sky together
like forsaken Greeks in some old tragedy
and he tells you things you never thought a person could

you have a secret dream of walking down the street holding hands
but shake it off like it's no big deal

you'll settle for the safety of a bedroom
or an empty train carriage
using the time in between stops to feel his lips
in total silence

before him there were things you knew
for sure
things that you could trust
but ever the boy you've come to terms
with becoming the man you know you must

rest safe in the knowledge   nothing can be learnt
until everything you thought to be true
has been broken   left to rust

old woman #2

ring   ring   ring   ring

    hello? is that you   ?

    hi am I speaking to   ?

              who's asking?

    it's   here from   we're calling today

              tonight it's tonight it's the middle of
              the night

    well   Mrs   I'm actually calling tonight because I was
    wondering
    if you are happy with your current   provider?

    Mrs   are you still there?

    Mrs   ?

              oh fuck off

solitude is not the same as loneliness

that pitchy darkness
a weighted   heavy thing
that sits
pondering its own
blue heart
keeping itself awake
through the insomnia of inexpedient hours

hold tight
to who you are
leaking whole parts of yourself
while you wait it out
for the next new moon

this chaos of flesh
this crave to degrade ourselves
noise
noise
noise
and data

know that solitude is not the same as loneliness
learn to make the distinction
and practise it
it has been known to save lives

fear

bus stops deserted

train stations like a wasteland

street corners shunned

bridges forsaken

and no one carries umbrellas anymore
they're never out long enough
to get caught in the rain

go everywhere by car
back home before it gets dark

unpublished

headline print rubs off onto our hands
stains our lovers
blackens our children

empathy: chip paper for a yesterday that went unpublished

carer

1

wake up get Oli ready for school dressed
toast orange juice walk him to the crossing
for the school gates let him cross himself
big boy now he says says he doesn't wanna
go in with his mum says it's embarrassing
so I concede because he is always on time
for school I make sure of that

2

back here quick coffee
and a smoke try to wake up
then the bus to the home
day spent washing old men
one calls me a dirty nigger whore
says we voted
so people like you would be
sent back home
I say I'm from Birmingham

acquired brain injuries most of them are like vegetables
but some of them are violent men men bigger than me
stronger the ones who would really do some damage
have done damage some of the girls haven't got a clue
just do it part-time whilst they're at college they all
leave for Uni after a while though it's been ten years
now always told myself I wouldn't get stuck here but
then Oli came along

3

by the time I finish my shift he's in bed
walks back home alone recently although
I don't like it anything could happen
but I've gotta make it work somehow
he's a good lad sometimes he tries to stay up late
play his video games but most of the time he's no
trouble it's no life even if you've got money we're just
pawns on a chessboard really the only thing we can do
is make ripples in the water I think that's what
you've gotta do because it's all you can do but
I'm working all the time when I'm not working
I'm sleeping cause I'm so tired and I feel guilty
about Oli I think you're sleeping your life away
working these fucking shifts not designed for women although it's
basically only women working there old women young women women
who are carers anyway cause care's always left to women 'cause it seems
that men just don't care I've got a kid of my own
but no fuck him fuck Oli but I can never stop
because rent is never gonna stop is it?

4

Mum

                             yes darling

I'm scared

                             why honey?

bad dream

have you been playing those video
games again?

promise?

cause you're bound to get nightmares
playing them
they're not appropriate

blood   Mummy

Shush darling
come sit next to me
it's alright

blood
so much blood

ocean memo

these are ones dead of the land
not by the sea
washed to the shore

.

children

..

i wash them back to the lands that have failed them
ready to be buried in the space of a shallow headline

natural disaster

we find ourselves in merciless times
where compassion spends itself daily
on the hope its investment will see a return

and every fallen city is a never-ending reflection
of an empire that was never killed
only wounded

clouds littered with skyscrapers

atmosphere dense   clamouring

flags heavy   with blood and conquest

the patriots' anthem sings out in discord

a nameless soldier is killed for a country
that will never lay down its weapons

a daughter is unsewn by the men who only pick her up to pick her
apart

and a mother watches her city burn
a city that said goodbye long before it caught flame

and the youngest son
picks up a frenzied gun

and starts firing

tainted landscape

shattered glass bottles
spilling boats into the ocean

like a Turner landscape
all at sea

sharp as knives in your side
splintering into a thorn

a thousand lives break
in the tainted landscape

                              swarm
                              swarm

is that blood
or spilt paint?

little drops into the ocean
muddying the view in rhetoric

full stops in the water
ink in the empty space of mercy

but of course they will eventually cry for you child
tears—our bodies' natural defence to deter foreign bodies

the view from here

when the drones
       sometimes known as offences
              put the balance of day and night out of kilter
it will look as if the sky is on fire with a violent
    wrathful God

you'd be forgiven
for mistaking it for day
you're not from this place
how would you be expected to know?

buildings mushroom
   during 3.25 fajr
               apartments crumble
               to meet the parched ground
as if they contained water
   were returning to the earth to feed the famished soil
and a strange bark breaks out
     gives way to howling
           lurking around every corner
mothers with children still left alive
      shut their doors and windows to it
            in the hope it might
          stay far
it is a sound that most closely resembles
how an atom splits
and the shape of the word *collateral*
blood thickens around broken glass
   and sporadic violence
the day picks up its shattered dream   of yesterday's
   explosion
yet   the news camera does   nothing
but watch
        cold as dead stone

disease

all of these terrible happenings are symptomatic of the illness but they are not the illness itself

the illness lies deeper   buried within years of unexamined   rotten flesh

before

the sky even had a name
when it was just an upside down ocean
and birds were really fishes that did back-strokes in the water
when the night sky was something to marvel at
before the last star was sold to an oligarch
when the twilight would make you bow your head
and the sun followed you all day
concerned with the arc of your narrative
when you knew how to speak to animals
before two towers fell
before America raised the corpse of its culture
and set it on fire again
before we replaced religion for capitalism
before religion was used to enforce feudalism
before every body that fell looked like   you

breathless gods

onomatopoeic broken bones

exhausted bodies

shrieking from a thickset white man who shouts until he is red in the
face

the feeling that someone is walking over your grave when an officer
walks past you on the street

it could have been you

imaging the scenario

deciding that despite the trauma that
    if you were raped or badly beaten you'd at least
    be alive

physically

tree branches swing in the breeze
echo of Billie and Nina

equality a tired refrain never reaching its crescendo
delayed by a gunshot   or a straightjacket

an oft spoken platitude
hums incessantly

reminding you of these   our post-racial days

forgotten somewhere between yesterday's hashtag   and today's
newest trend

wings beat against a laboured skyline
as tomorrow becomes today
          and nothing much changes
ashes mix with coal station smoke
white tissues soak black particles
          in businessman's sneeze
          hand scrunches into a fist

cities coated in the fog of force and violence   brutalised bodies and
deadtoosoon

caged birds long for the majesty of flight from private prisons
anxious feet tread through institutionalised streets
heavy with ghosts of siblings

bodies breathe their last in blood and wasp-sting
whipped and beaten
klan robes traded for police badges

should i say names like statistics
or atrocities in history
when that would only serve to help you forget?

invoke their name like magic
to curse houses and businesses built rich
with lynch and plantation money

i won't

i don't get to use their name in poetry

it is blasphemy to a god

i will leave them now to heaven
to reap the beauty that our intolerance crushed

there are no graves in the sky
only oceans heavy with storm-clouds

                                            sons   daughters
                                            mothers   fathers
                                            aunties   uncles
                                            children
                                                            of richer suns

i will let them to heaven now
and wait for our fate to unfold

fallen leaves

bodies fall to the earth
like autumn were forever
does anything even
matter anymore?
all this loss

everywhere everything   everyone

with a poem i only have the poem
but within it is
everywhere
    everything
        everyone

i see everywhere is lost   to the everything
that effects

grind

young men and women grind their days away in offices and come out
in the sunset of their age
bleached of their youth   all those stolen years
young men and women go into offices
    factories warehouses
and come to graveyards
    cold

if in paradise

every third thought is of earth
does that explain why in the City
i can do nothing but think of hell?

banker

no rest for the wicked because   the wicked never rest can't take my
fingers off the pulse of London because this city is my city and it always
has been always will be money talks and if you haven't got money then
no one will hear you scream   I do get afraid sometimes   it used
to be that I didn't sleep cause I didn't want to sleep but now I can't
just sit   watching the clock and that scares me
because   only The Devil doesn't sleep and I'm worried I
     IIII might just be The Devil honestly I'll catch my reflection in
the mirror and I'll look contorted and monstrous and I'll think to
myself   that's your soul right in front of you mate
I've done terrible things such terrible terrible things
during the day I don't think about them but can't   help but think
about them when the day is done

false profit

we must unite

hold hands to shake the old plantation house

bloated big business
the banks
these temples where the false profit
of Capital and Coin are worshipped daily

we tend to their altars uphold their scripture of
    The Self
giving them our time
our hours   our lives

        the soles are worn from our shoes

                our coats too thin

as these devils grow fat
off what we give so freely

anarchist

I sleep remarkably well all things considered
I usually dream of clouds
white fluffy clouds
resting safely in the knowledge that everything's going to burn

late afternoon

the last of a half-drunk coffee cup sits alone
little wisps of steam rising above it
before it evaporates
turns to cold water

my neighbour half-strums a guitar
in the late afternoon
and when the notes stop
vibrating
    i think that must be the space in his life
        since his wife died

school closes its oft-read   tired white textbook
the kids traipse out
reclaim the streets
in a flood of rude voices
laughter and sugar

old men and women wait for buses under shelters
take refuge from the day's disappointment

while men in suits whizz past
press cold beach shells close to their ear
like they held secrets from the ocean

cash machines bleep
vape pens are sucked
trains glitch momentarily
a text hesitates to send

a cloud masks the sunlight
ends the interval
                to stars

and the sky finally gives way
                which can't be seen
                over the fumes

departure gate

I know what you're thinking
      rat leaving sinking ship
      you may well be right
except
      not really rat leaving sinking ship

rat leaving sinking ship that is on fire
sinking ship that is sinking backwards
      backwards into the past

old woman #3

I had dreams
I had ambitions
I don't know where they've gone

sometimes I go looking for them
in the back of cupboards when I'm dusting
but I only find old tins of baked beans

winter

the winter wraps the country in its icy grip and
    freezes those too poor to heat their homes
tramps are transformed to statues by suddenly shocked
    blood

later   when the archaeologists come to excavate this
      fallen city
they'll think we prayed to them
left coppers [now rusted]
in reverence to these saints and minor deities

they'll think we worshipped each one

eviction

1

that's it then couldn't afford it so I had to leave   not that I would have
paid anyway

it's the principle of the matter   this city is coming apart at the seams
    I've been ripped clean

out of it

let's make no bones about it that flat was a shithole
but it was my shithole

    streets stink reeks rotten meat maggots writhing around in the
fresh kill

that's us waste in the refuge truck of this city   I'm sick of it   broken
down overpriced   clapped out sell it back

why the fuck should I have to leave 'cause a greedy landlord wants to
raise his rents?

raises them sky-high 'cause there ain't no safe-guard   no one is
looking out for people like me

all for some briefcase wanker who wants to live closer to the nearest
tube

2

walk through the streets with my bin bags like a refugee

I've become one of the people I used to walk past

but I want someone to notice   I'm screaming

can anyone please help me

everyone's just walking or ignoring me I know they can hear me

they're just choosing to ignore it'll come   come for them though

it's coming for all of them

coming for you too

3

the streets are full of rubbish all your kids are either on pills or watching
porn

that's the truth mayaswell tell you as it is and the destruction

      but no one speaks about the destruction because if you don't
      talk about it

it might go away but it isn't going anyway the ice-caps are melting

the ozone layer is a huge bleeding wound in the sky and Britain is
broken

      do it up and sell it on again for a stupid price Britain benefits
      Britain blame it on whoever is suffering most Britain

      this country makes my breath stink

4

mister hipster
how many kebab shops have you converted into
   wineries?
how many squats have become flats none of us can
   afford
how many people have been displaced
re-housed

delivered clean
from your sterile   up and coming
white neo-liberal
individualism

do you feel cool surrounded by poor people?
do you not see that if your answer is yes
the poor are dying
and you are the sickness

mister hipster
do you not know
that the walls of your luxury tenement flat are dense
with angry   righteous ghosts?

funeral

the fresh upturned soil
unkind
      because it looked so rich

the branches   departed from the rest of the day
outside the traffic still moved
birds still sang

nothing stopped
      the way it's supposed to

the space between what exists
and that which fertilises clear

it lay before us all
as we stared down
at the shallow opening
like a hole a child might dig in the sand at the beach
before climbing out
when the tide rolls in

within it
and all across the burial plot
hundreds of stories
that have since gone untold
added to the soil
made the grave
the richest place

first funeral flowers
withered in the frost
never to be replaced

in bed in your flat (holding your gaze)

your voice was soft
the smoke made my eyes smart
we were curled under your sheets

maybe you thought i was being coy
in reality i've just always hated my body

you kept your window open
outside London was dying
the air heavy with its pretence and shining bullshit

there was me thinking i was going to be an anarchist
and wreak havoc
but now i am lost in your curls

i've got your face memorised
and i'm standing on the other side of myself
    —watching the view

you are the softest of revolutions
the only one worth living through

months later

remembering that kiss that shape of jaw
that smoothness of skin   how your lips
linger longer than is necessary

and now i'm burning again
now i'm that ash we rubbed fast
  from your sheets in case it set them on fire
                              now i am that fire
burning everything in my path

you are tracing the shape of my face
brushing away the dark places
taking me over so completely
leading me to some place new

you

you made me realise what the crook in a man's neck was there for
you made me realise what a body was for
you made me think if this is all that there is
then maybe this could be enough
more than enough

Love and Desire

Desire looks at Love's profile really wants to fuck him
Love's had his heart broke too many times before   Love is a
Cancer   the star sign not the disease (although it's open to
interpretation)

Love is a deeply emotional being   prone to get attached
     Desire is a millennial through and through doesn't label anything
     refuses to label
or be labelled other than the label of
     I thought we weren't putting a label on this?

Love finds himself constantly unhappy confused by this tendency
of never being honest
Love has this feeling that he doesn't often speak
a feeling that sends him weak at the knees
makes him blush in front of the cynics seem naïve

that sex is never really casual that whether you like it or not if
you're attracted to someone   on some level somewhere some part
of you is imagining some kind of future with that person

Desire thinks that's a load of bollocks   that this begotten notion of
monogamy has been bequeathed by our patriarchal forefathers
and he may be rightbut he only ever says this when he's out to
impress

the arrogant arc of Desire cock-sure swinging his limbs grinning
wildly
espousing on   instant gratification no strings attached

Desire is so over this emotional nonsense   Desire's had a lot of
partners   one night stands Tinder Grindr for him this is all that
there is all that there needs to be

But Love is feeling like the age he lives in is out to kill him   Desire
seems so hard-boiled   so rough
Love can't deny there's something he finds attractive
 in him   Love himself feels a certain Lust or Desire for Desire
    which is complicated
but there is this terrible part they cannot reconcile with he doesn't
really like him   there is just this primitivism between them of
flesh on flesh of tongue tasting every part   devouring
then this feeling so terrible like Love had never been satisfied

so Love shuts it down deletes the dick pics   deletes his account
    and waits

Friday night now   three drinks and a half a pill in
there he is clutching a fag in the smoking area looking out over the
fog   with tired   puffy eyes
holding out hope that the next one might be the one
the one good man that he can Trust

when the last bomb falls on love

when the sun shrinks to a cinder
and the last bomb falls on love
just before your heart stops beating
you'll hear the fluttering of a dove

you'll hear its wings thrashing
like daybreak
tear across the burning sky
you'll hear its long-lost birdsong
and you will ask yourself why

is it only at the end
when we have squandered this earth to nothing
when we have burned the last drop of oil
drained the ocean dry
that we realise what we could have had
the way things might have been
if we had been kinder
and gone about things differently

scourge

i don't remember the last time i wrote
these days i can't seem to make out
the words from the empty spaces

the only thing i could write
would be the poem that told you
of how beautiful i think you are

and the tragedy that you have forgotten

the only thing keeping me from the railway tracks
are my friends and family

the injustice the inordinate wealth of a tiny few over the many the
terror the anger this fury this ancient restless tongue this need to
speak to seek out a meaning an answer faced with a lifetime of
ceaseless barbarism questioning the point of existence and the
ultimate futility of art

skin

and yet—
somehow
it has resisted all this
it has survived

on the day capitalism met its death

the poets were defunct there was no one left to heal
commuters abandoned tube stations re-discovered light
phones were cast aside   books picked up
guns were buried in the ocean like sunken ships
flags felt ashamed   spontaneously combusted
as borders unbolted   fell apart
the slaughterhouse abolished
meant animals roamed the earth once more
as private prisons were sacked
schools revolutionised
cashpoints uncoupled
and politicians big business men   fascists
    editors   monarchs   judges   journalists
oppressors of all trades
finally knew what it meant to be stripped to the bone
to have everything you have ever loved   and cherished
stolen from you

moving forward

an old bench atop a high point of the city
where you take in the whole grey view
nothing   but steel echoes

above a sinking sky
forming a passing grace
saving a lonely man or woman from indifference
respite at least from loneliness
as the atmosphere splutters above us

for when i find myself most alone
wandering the city like a lost pup

i always seem to find you
revealing some intimate part of myself
i had hidden away
in order to keep safe

craving wind on a stifled day
looking at how rotten the city looks from up here

i am always the person i'd never imagined myself to be
    by now
but when everything looks like an ending
and my heart throws itself
against my ribcage
lamenting

and i am consumed with nothing but the worst facets of
    the human
i find you
at a train station
or a bus stop

at a cash point   reeling
dissolving back into the ocean
holding all of the love
and that which is real
in your mass

i meet you
i pass by you
exchange words
a smile
a glance

and on days like this
it is enough

time pushes forward resolute
man pushes his boulder like Sisyphus
Cassandra utters prophecies
that fall on deaf earphones

but you
in the middle of a city
at separates

make me feel whole enough
to keep moving forward

error 404

each time you allow yourself to love
indiscriminately
a device freezes
an algorithm glitches
a software update
hesitates

the soft man

the soft man waits to be born
in the womb of a punched wall
                                    wishing
he could somehow speak quietly
could sing through the ages
recall the stories from childhood
that told of a boy like him

so that people would say
his way was familiar
that it did not threaten manhood
but encouraged a new growth
an unlearning of slate flesh

no man is a temple

so why would he build himself
out of stone?

to unlock freedom
bring back spring from its diverted path
the stone must allow itself to be eroded

he must unpick the barbed wire from his skin
must flow in time with the currents of the ocean
and not against them

to get back what has been lost
            what was stolen
            what was soft
            tender and pink
            at birth

he must first de-construct
learn to see the sun in the sky

and not gold to pillage
not women   land   fortunes to claim

mother to himself
lover to himself
fights those who would destroy
the intricate coat he'd make for himself

a coat that would weather storms
warm against graveyards
that would grow rich off the magnificent art
he would offer to the earth in his rot
if he never reached the summit of himself

for a softer (that is to say freer) man to be born
the colours in his dream must be rich
he must allow himself to spill like sands
he must seek out a leaf from his sister's struggles
verse himself well in their plight

learn that what suffocates women
strangles him too and entombs his body
in a dull copper statue
of some bygone tyrant

man must unpick himself
like stitches around a festering wound
and start again

a radical peace

i feel a radical peace beyond the smoke of rhetoric
its dawning

i can feel a new day about to break
we hold close to hope
no matter how bleak things seem
because it's the only thing that keeps us here

singing low in the streetlights
way after chuckout time on a Friday night
looking up from the sick on the chewing-gum pumiced
    pavements

seeing the infinite sky
and knowing
there is more to life
than what we've reduced life to

we were not meant to live like this

it is gathering

inexorable as nature

slow as history

consciousness

a peace every living thing is born with
the only true entitlement of all life

getting back all that was pure and sacred at birth
before it was perverted   misshapen to hatred

nothing is born ignorant
beings learn ignorance

from their peers
or their parents
or their society

but freedom
freedom for all things
all things that live

it is in you
can't you hear it   singing?

quick!
stifle it before you realise

kill it before it speaks

it must be getting nearer
we're the most awake we've ever been
(which isn't much by the state of things)
but might just be enough

feel the urge that won't settle in your chest
feel that urgent dream that keeps you from your rest
that shakes the core of your conformity
as each injustice robs you
leaves you bleeding

see—every day you walk the streets and feel you're the only one
truly living

i've felt this too

but rarely spoke it

so seek me out

and remember when life gets darkest and you wrestle

with that voice and the only thing that stops you   from ending
yourself is the thought of your friends   family your job your house
your mortgage

know there is so much more

and in reality what really keeps you from doing it
is all those times before
you thought the world had ended
but still   somehow   for better   or for worse
just   kept   going

life is eternal
we bequeath
parents beget
i gave birth to this
we are all just making connections
and i hope this reaches you in time

life is made rich by the quality of your love
life is empathy
poetry is empathy
love is radical

love destroys a machine because a machine cannot love
    only simulate love
and the simulation of love
is a poor reproduction

if you feel that it's true: then it is

if you live it: it happens

everywhere you will ever go is thick with the history and
    future of all that has been and all that is yet to come
feel it in the reeling cities
in the surging tides

know that there are oncoming storms to weather
know that you live in uncertain days
but to stay kind stay loving stay alive
means staying together
question politics
question business
question those who do not question
but follow blindly

every last breath
first cry
unjust bullet
unused life
lingers
soaked up by the landscape

peace is in you
no matter how ugly this world has made you
rattling the cages of your politicised heart

the essential human truth
the thing that makes you human

is that nothing is alien
no thing is alien

and those who rebuke the sentiment
have vested interests (usually financial   always political)

and every act of violence that you condone
or look away from is an act of complicity
which negates your innocence

live the tomorrow that you dream of
the one's poets wrestle with writing
lest they sound naïve

tomorrow is here

if you want it to be
a tiny act can spark the greatest of revolutions

and yes
the blood flows
bodies fall
love is poisoned
politicised
Britain is rotting
and America is on fire
but if these things are spoken
then they are fought

silence has always been the greatest weapon
of the oppressor
apathy is a cancer of the soul
we should all take measures to prevent

we are not born evil
we are not born good
we are born human
prone to be led by the basest of our desires
and to carry on the way things are without thinking

we find ourselves in a cruel and unjust
power structure that is out of control

it must be dismantled
and replaced with one that is kinder
one that knows how to support and nourish
its most vulnerable

william blake said every thing is holy
he was right
every thing is holy and everyone deserves to live life and not a
sentence

the intersections of oppression show to some extent we are all of us
maligned in this construction site of The Self
it is simply the question of to what extent
and how we must remedy the damage already done
to counter the infringements of to our personal freedoms
in the hope the days ahead will be tender

"it's a beautiful thing, the destruction of words"—1984, George Orwell

~~empathy~~
~~empathy~~
~~empathy~~
~~empathy~~
~~empathy~~
~~empathy~~
~~empathy~~
~~empathy~~
~~empathy~~
~~empathy~~
~~empathy~~
~~empathy~~
~~empathy~~
~~empathy~~
~~empathy~~
~~empathy~~
~~empathy~~
~~empathy~~

the committee for the defence against terrorism

and radicalisation found
[after a lengthy dossier on the matter
and thousands in public spending]

that language
particularly the manipulation
inversion and degradation of language

to be the most effective way
to wage the next wave
in the war on terror

language to bind and disembody
to cut off the tongue of the uneducated
leave them speechless
replace it with something new
steel   lacerated edges
dipped in acid

language as the perfect incubus
a breeding ground for binaries

language to rebirth the scapegoat of the hour
preserve that which is established
that which is accepted
conventional
lauded

language to [redacted]
language to [censored]
language to [explicit content]
language to [sensitive material]

language to torture free speech

towering inferno

if you are unfortunate to have been born poor
then I am afraid you will burn
but you do have the privilege of dying next to
    Notting Hill's premium luxury apartments

if you're lucky enough to stay alive however
and since the journalists are kicking up a fuss
you may just be rehoused
in the symbol that saw your plastic
working class façade
burn to the ground

and there will be a charity single recorded for you
for everyone to listen
and weep at

if you are poor
if you are not white
if you just do not matter
please
die quietly

but remember
this is a tragedy
so don't get angry
you don't get to be angry over a tragedy

you must be sad
you must weep
only   weep more quietly

fading light

days fade
   news breaks
never stops
     but i've forgotten
         everything else

no use for truth
     when truth is worthless
     worthless bitcoin breaks my heart

there is so much beauty everywhere
     but the light is fading fast
watching the night draw in from up here
     every sunset looks like the last

pathetic fallacy (everything's okay)

look outside your window—see the storm raging—know the
weather is mother nature's emotions—remember how at school you
learned that the writer's choice of weather foreshadowed plot—
imbued tone

tell yourself it's nothing
that there is nothing wrong   anywhere
everything's okay
           but she is furious

ask yourself why
tell yourself it'll be alright

the girl you work with has a boyfriend who's started getting visions

became vegan
switched to alkaline foods
read more
fell deep into the dark-net
until the light was spent

started meditating
meditated until that space between sleep and wake narrowed
and she said the way the light found him showed him something
new

and she talks of how he walks the streets terrified someone's going
to take him

worries he'll wake one day on a slab
being dissected

there's something he's read
linking the pineal gland and his melanin

when it first happened he was in his room
his eyes began to fog
he thought he was going blind

straining from beneath his lids
something was approaching
crawling underneath his eyes

then it came

the shadows formed shapes
shapes merged into colours
then pictures
he pushed himself

squinted hard
until he thought his eyes
would pop out

and then
there
right there
some new
dark vision grew

are you ok baby?

    yeah
    yeah
    I'm fine

    it's nothing

    it's nothing

        except

business as usual

the winds   will change

          the tides   will turn

     the papers   will predict the worse

                         at first   we'll blame God
                         and then   terrorists

                         who've finally succeeded
                         in turning the sky against us

the names of hurricanes will chill parental bones
mothers will whisper them into the ears of their young
like childhood monsters

the waters will withdraw
from Britain's banks
churn and circle
like a pack of ravenous wolves
fighting over the last   bone

                    before they burst their banks
                    reduce cities to myth
                    and still
                    we won't be convinced

we will live in the solitude
of our newfound sovereignty
our buildings reaching higher than God
soaring like Icarus in the glory of our new empire's sun

and we will stare into the screen

so we don't hear the planet's scream

meanwhile the prophets will rage into pages ofdigitalised poetry
[before being censored]

research papers of disgraced postgrads
will be vindicated
pass into platitude and proverb

no one will enter a building without an escape plan
no one will enter a building without an escape plan

the oceans will boil
curdle to milk
as landmass
returns
to the sea

words such as
unexpected   unprecedented
freak extreme
will become
obsolete

those foolish enough to still swim will blister and crack
                           burned by the sulphur
the few tribes left alive   will die of the water
those too poor to afford gas masks
                           will die of the air

crops will fail
villagers perish
ice will burn
to gas
        fires break out spontaneously

reclaim the forests starved by drought

and the children
will soak up the view with their tiny terrified eyes
the first words of the newborn uncurling itself
between the bloodied effluent
of its mother's legs will be
is this the future you left me?

but still
amidst all this chaos
we will not blame ourselves
or the part that we have played
collectively   to total the sum
of our capital's violence

so
it'll be business as usual in Britain
we will frack and burn and bleed
unmoved by our destruction
as Nature prostrated on her knees
shouts curses to the pylons
and the men who murdered all her trees
this our mountainous inhumanity
to feed our never-ending greed

nothing to see

ravens will shun withered branches flock to the boardrooms
observe the final act in the farce of the human
zoom in   watch as the fall into the sea
caw at one another as the city
drops   to its knees

and the ocean
like a swollen womb
grown heavy with the miscarriage of our
days will bleed

how did this happen?
the people will utter
weeping in the gutter
as the hospitals
bolted and shuttered
forced to close their doors
to all with poor credit scores

underfed nauseous following orders
the patriots will sing Rule   Britannia
between mouthfuls of garbled salt water
we need stronger borders
they will say
before the tide rolls in
and washes them away

closed eyed to the omens
            listening to the
moneymen the earth lies reeling
                democracy—a shallow
dream ignore what you've broken
            forget what was stolen

for this City to rise

and poison the sky with

tell yourself

there is nothing to see

because they never thought it would come to their town
carried on   kept their heads bowed from the sky
but when it ripped   roared   like a wounded animal
there was no denying
thick   black   liquid-   like ink
rolled in fast
in the blink of an eye

the sky blackened   like a dead laptop screen
matched the furious water's rage
destroyed whole towns as it came
gushing from the shore
still the politicians
played their war-games

the people didn't care until it was their kids   their home
washed clean from the earth in the last of the landslides
carried off in the mouth of an unkind tide

a foreigner now   in some distant place
where the people   seem unkind
a refugee displaced

no money for foreign aid
they will say
your boat gets spun round
your kids pushed away

sharks in the water
   wolves at your door
       turning your gaze
           from a full-force
              gale and a rising tide
fast—
        avert your eyes

because these are the end times
nothing left
but magpie-eyed men
with corporate sponsors
scouring the earth for the last coin
the one patch of unclaimed soil
to re-develop
and sell on again

frack   bleed
    oil oil
Syria weeping in drone-struck rubble
capitalist terrorism
      frack   privatise
burn burn baby
   develop
      colonise

strong and stable
the latest jingle rings like a tired download

strong and stable

weak and unconvincing

Britain just a clod
apart from the continent
sinking

so—

slam your door

hammer a border sign into the earth

no entry
no foreigners

sorry [fuck off] *we're full*

turn your back on all that you started
look away from the war-torn
discarded lands

sever ties
dissolve unions
divorce all that needs you
and calls for your help
as it cries for its mother

torn   fractured   fragmented

like broken English
spoken in the mouth
of some dying foreign tongue

water

    distance

        widening frictions

shredded tongues

        and media fictions

stolen language

  bloody money

      old colonial sea-monster surveillance

          polices

      Trojan gifts

enemies within

      an explosion hits

widens the rift

    false profit

  blind profit

        over-time

    and many losses

bastardised eyes

       and heavy hearts

and borders

    and borders

and borders

    and bombs

    and borders

                and borders

    and borders

    and bombs and

           borders

    and borders and borders

    and bombs and borders

    and borders and borders and

slow fade

hungry kid   no food at lunch
student can't afford their textbooks

a pensioner freezing in her bungalow
a listless beggar in his cardboard home

can't walk   fit for work
sanctioned   incapacitated

a nurse heading home from a late shift
bleary-eyed   unappreciated

privatise privatise
privatise in quiet

maybe if you distract the hopeless they may not even notice

until there is nothing left of what was said to make this   Nation great
anything to get the scroungers out their beds

blame it on the Muslims
blame it on the Pious

blame it on maniacal religious devotion

better yet   blame it on the refugees
sinking in the ocean
blame whoever best suits the current cultural scape-goat of the moment

whoever can take the strain of our collective   fickle hate

demonise as you do it
say you're keeping your Great Nation safe

let us be at separates
let us stand apart
easier to police divided
than if we stand as one

we are flammable and eggshell frail
no one can talk without shouting

the tower blocks are burning
the streets are overcrowded

fear and uncertainty holds us tight within its grip
the meek shall inherit the earth   what about your kids?

racist chants
and shallow platitudes
and Britain's new found solitude

this distance that we share
seems to magnify   enlargen
spreads its jaws a little wider
splurges   and engulfs us

the poor are getting poorer
families are starving
the animals   the vulnerable   the Left and the left behind are all dying

newspapers preying on every tragedy
posit that is them and this is us
rhetoric and frenzied headlines
surveillance policies and welfare cuts

oh look around and you will see it
the stability is staggering
but stare a little longer
and you can see it all
                    unravelling